We Are Here

Dona Herweck Rice

Consultant

Sean Goebel, M.S.
University of Hawaii
Institute for Astronomy

Publishing Credits

Rachelle Cracchiolo, M.S.Ed., *Publisher*
Conni Medina, M.A.Ed., *Managing Editor*
Diana Kenney, M.A.Ed., NBCT, *Senior Editor*
Dona Herweck Rice, *Series Developer*
Robin Erickson, *Multimedia Designer*
Timothy Bradley, *Illustrator*

Image Credits: Cover, p.1 NASA; p.5 AF archive / Alamy; pp.7, 8, 10, 16, 17, 20, 22, 24, 26 iStock; pp.28, 29 J.J. Rudisill; pp.2, 4, 11, 13, 14, 19, 20, 21, 22, 23, 31, 32 NASA; pp.7, 14, 15, 16, 17 Timothy J. Bradley; all other images from Shutterstock.

Library of Congress Cataloging-in-Publication Data

Rice, Dona, author.
We are here / Dona Herweck Rice.
pages cm
Summary: "Humans are like a tiny speck compared to Earth. And Earth is like a tiny speck compared to the universe. Words cannot describe how massive our universe really is. It's difficult to imagine that we're really so small. Even though we might be small compared to the universe, we are still part of this complex and fascinating system."-- Provided by publisher.
Audience: Grades 4 to 6
Includes index.
ISBN 978-1-4807-4687-9 (pbk.)
1. Cosmology--Juvenile literature. I. Title.
QB983.R54 2016
523.1--dc23

2014045210

Teacher Created Materials
5301 Oceanus Drive
Huntington Beach, CA 92649-1030
http://www.tcmpub.com

ISBN 978-1-4807-4687-9

Table of Contents

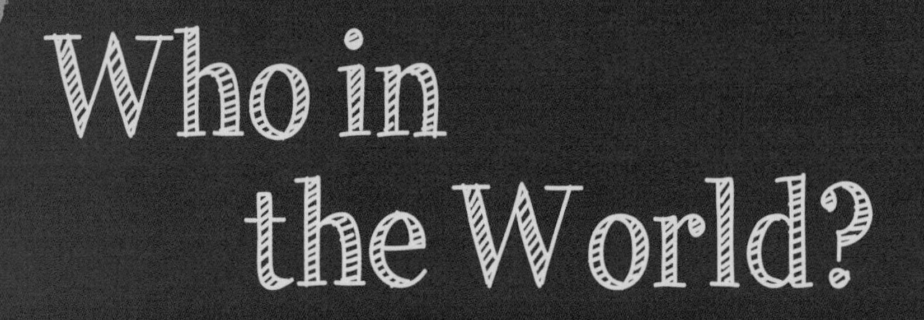

Who in the World?

In the world of Dr. Seuss, all the tiny Whos live in Whoville. Whoville lies deep within a dust speck resting on a small flower on planet Earth. Imagine what the Whos would think if they had any idea of the size of the world beyond their own! Imagine what it might be like to be just a tiny speck *on* a speck, smaller than the eye can see. The Whos only know their world. But there's more than they can imagine beyond where they can see.

The truth is, a Who's world view is not much different from our view here on Earth. In fact, even compared to just our galaxy, we're a lot smaller than any Who. Imagine what we look like compared to the **universe**!

Billions and Billions

Our sun is just one of at least 200 billion stars in the Milky Way galaxy. And the Milky Way is estimated to be one of at least 100 billion galaxies in the universe!

We live in the Milky Way galaxy.

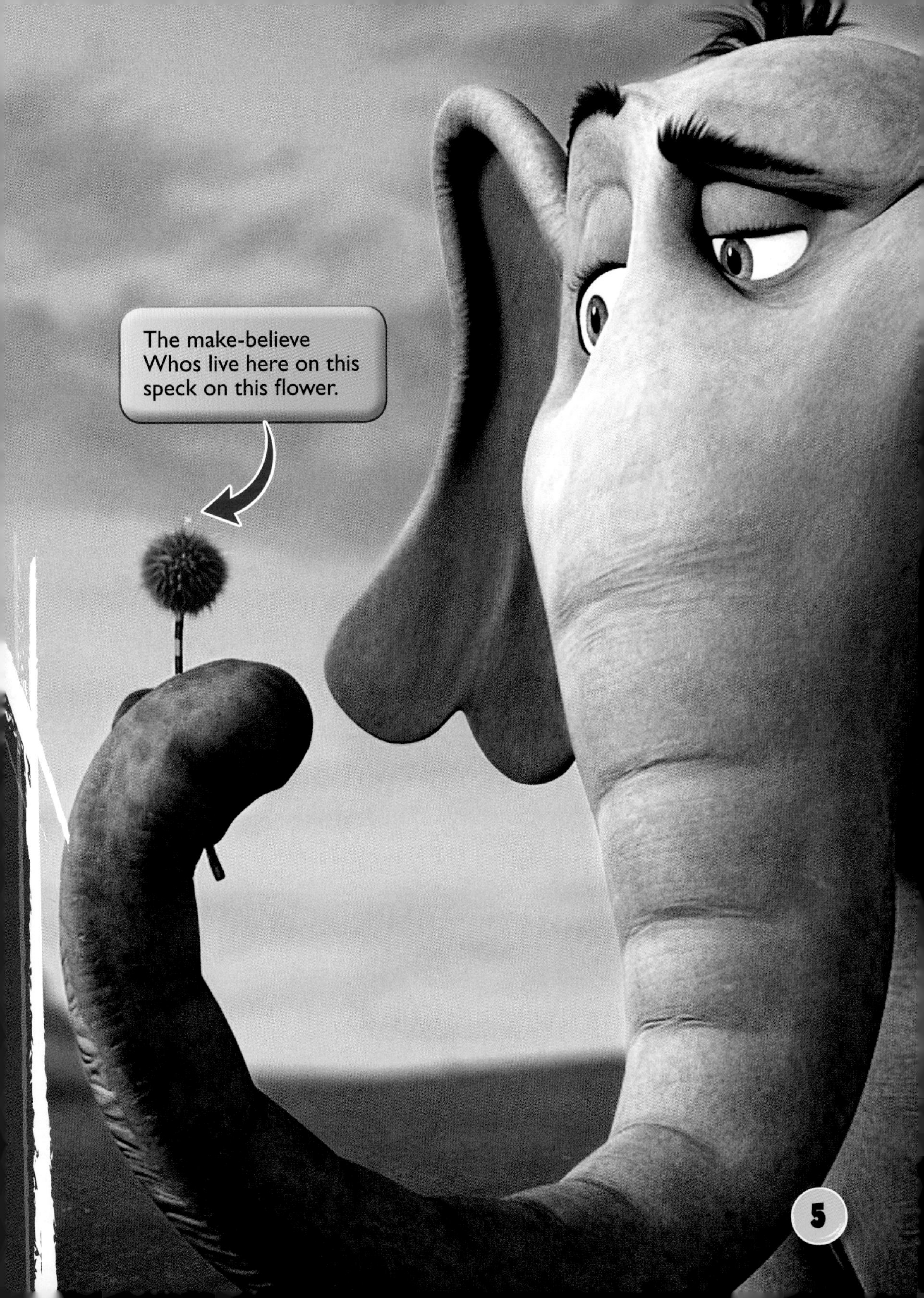
The make-believe Whos live here on this speck on this flower.

How Big Is Space?

We all know that space is big. But just how big is it?

Do you remember Buzz Lightyear calling out, "To **infinity** and beyond"? He was right. Space is infinite! Scientists think there aren't any borders to space. And the universe is **expanding** all the time.

Everything in the world you see around you has a beginning and an end. Look at your big toe. It only takes up so much space. Your body has skin to mark its limits. Earth is about 40,000 kilometers (25,000 miles) around its middle. The distance between Earth and the sun is about 150 million km (93 million mi.). But the distance from the sun to the edge of the universe? Let's just say you can't get there. Ever. There is no "there" there. Space goes on forever and ever and ever and ever and ever and...you get the idea.

Hello!

Hello!

It takes 8 minutes and 20 seconds for light to reach Earth from the sun.

Scientists say that the entire universe once existed in a tiny, single point in space.

Our Little Corner of the Universe

The space that we know best is the space closest to home. It's our own solar system.

Our solar system has eight planets. They **revolve** around our sun. There are also many moons that **orbit** the planets. **Dwarf planets**, such as Pluto and Eris, orbit the sun, too.

Eris is the dwarf planet farthest from the sun. It's about 68 AUs from the sun. Do the math! That means it's over 10 billion km (6 billion mi.) away. But as far away as Eris is, it doesn't even come close to the edge of our own solar system.

Astronomical Unit

Sizes in space are so vast that using kilometers and miles to measure distance isn't practical. Instead, we use the astronomical unit (AU). An AU is the average distance from Earth to the sun—about 150 million km (93 million mi.).

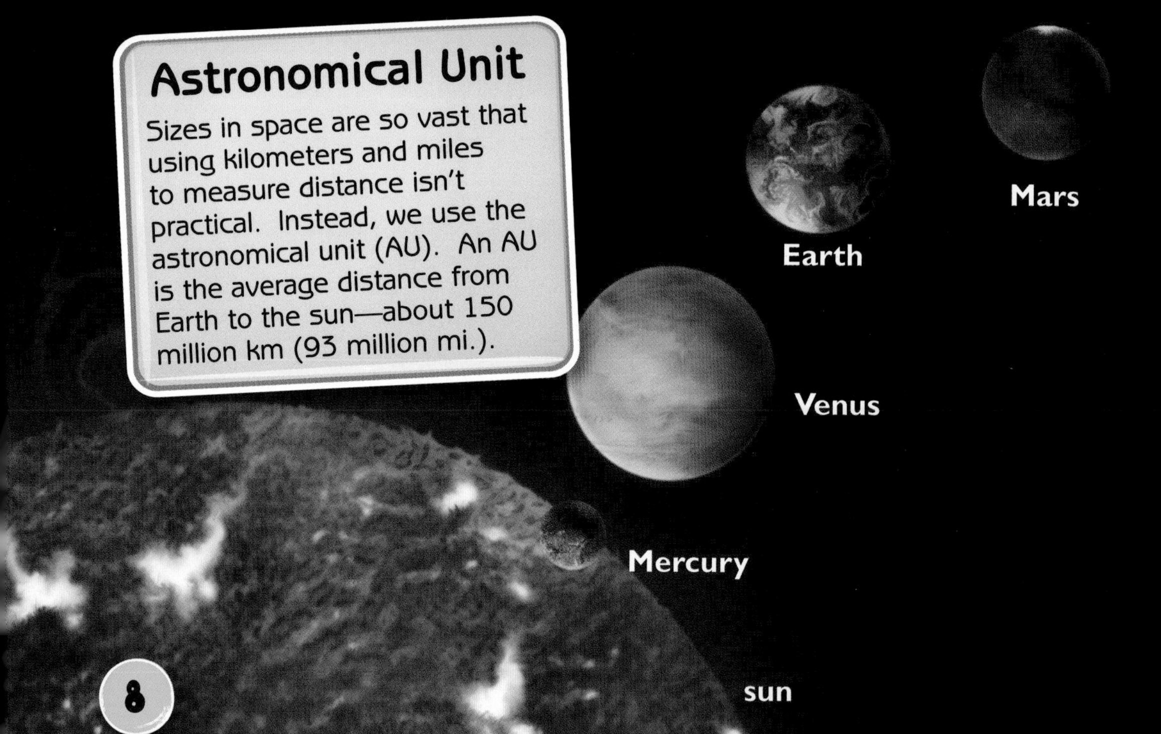

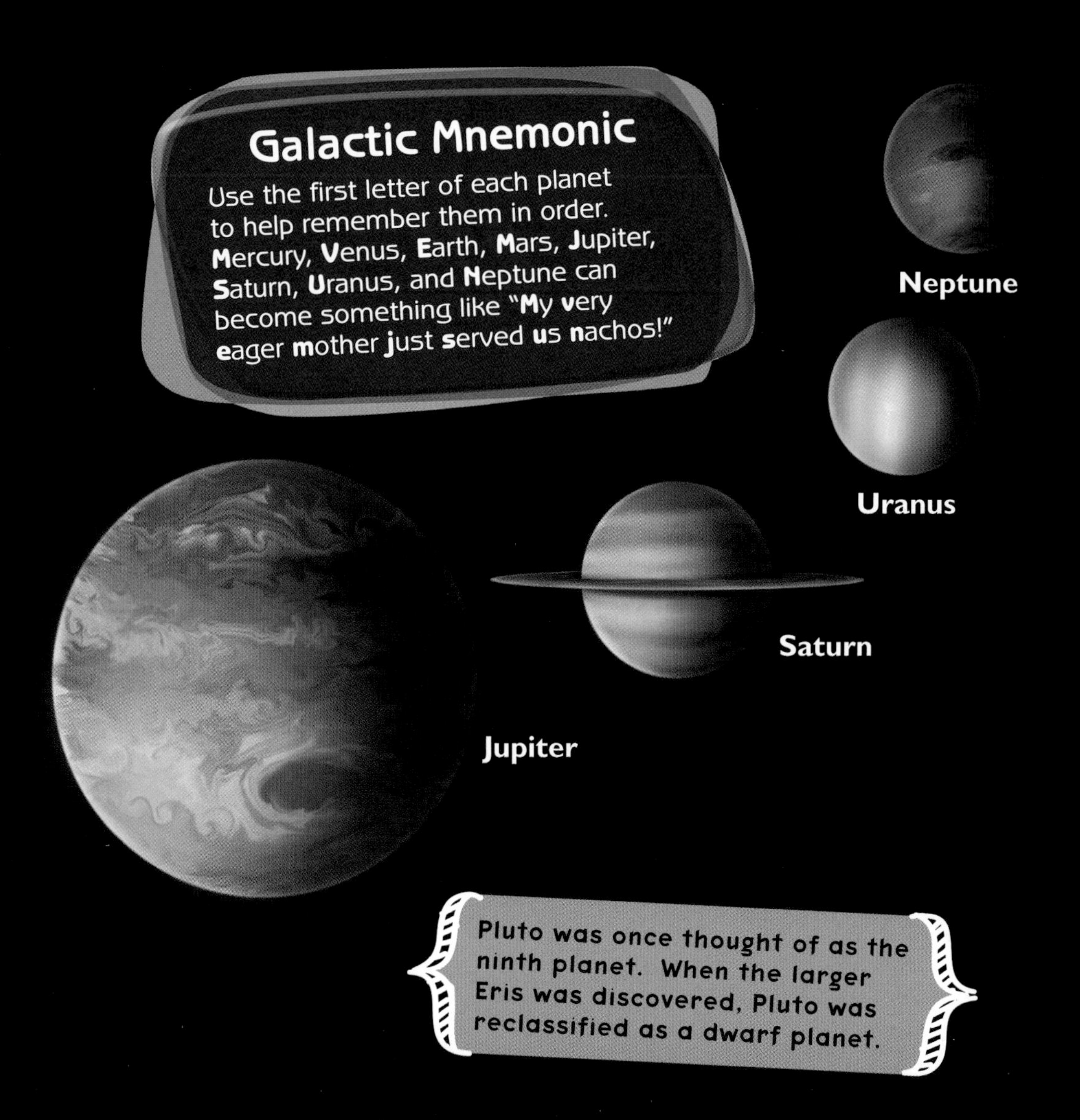

Pluto was once thought of as the ninth planet. When the larger Eris was discovered, Pluto was reclassified as a dwarf planet.

Our solar system includes everything within the sun's **gravity**. Gravity is a force that pulls. Earth moves through space at super-fast speeds. But we stick to its surface. We don't fly off or fall over like you might think we would. That's because of gravity. Everything in our solar system is there because of gravity from our massive sun.

Our Sun

Earth seems pretty big to us. But it's nothing compared to the sun. *Massive* is a good word to describe our sun. *Humongous* will also do. Nearly 1.3 million Earths would fit inside our sun!

Can you believe that, compared to other stars, our sun is really no big deal? Stars are **classified** by size, temperature, and color. Our sun is about 5,500° Celsius (10,000° Fahrenheit) at the surface. That's hot, of course. But it's only average for a star. The distance around the sun is about 4.4 million km (2.7 million mi.). That's big! But then again, it's not big for a star.

Our sun may not be super-sized. It may not be super-hot compared to all the other stars. But to our solar system and everything in it, the sun is the biggest deal around!

Polaris

Polaris, or the North Star, is actually a triple star system in the Little Dipper constellation. The primary star, Polaris A, is six times as massive as our sun.

Little Dipper

Kochab
Pherkad
Ahfa
Polaris
Yildun
Urodelus
Anwar

Scientists classify stars with a code to compare them with one another. Our sun is a G2V star.

Kuiper Belt

Let's get back to Pluto and Eris. They, along with other dwarf planets, are found in the Kuiper (KAHY-per) Belt. This is a wide area that circles the sun and planets the same way a belt circles a waist. It's made mainly of icy and rocky objects. The area extends about 50 AUs from the sun. That's a distance that's hard for our brains to imagine, especially since most adults never live more than a few kilometers from where they were born!

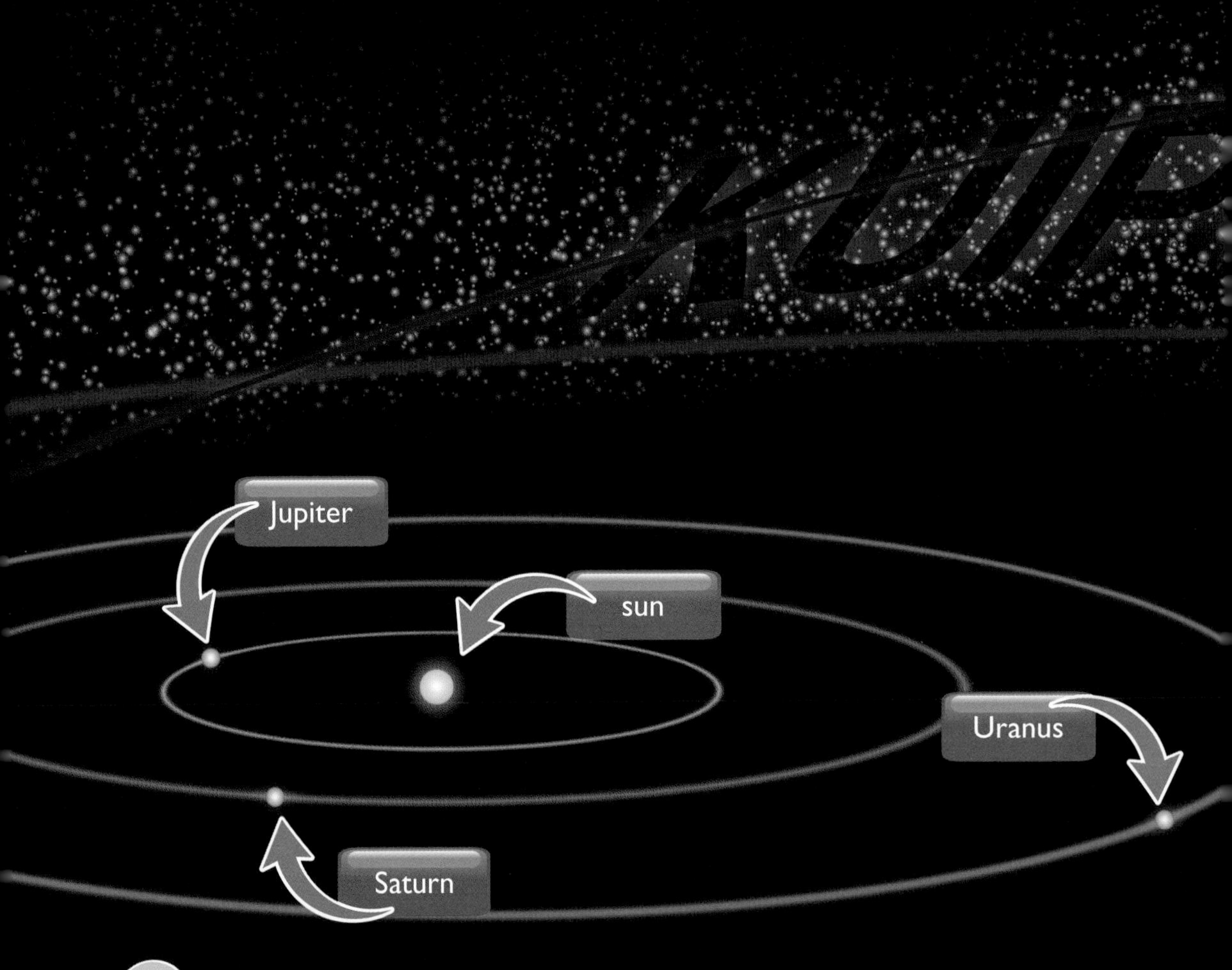

But the Kuiper Belt is still not the edge of our solar system. Beyond the Kuiper Belt is a huge area that extends from about 80 AUs to more than 200 AUs called the *heliosphere*. Here, strong solar winds pick up **matter** from space. The mass they create reaches to about 230 AUs from the sun.

But *that's* not the edge of our solar system either!

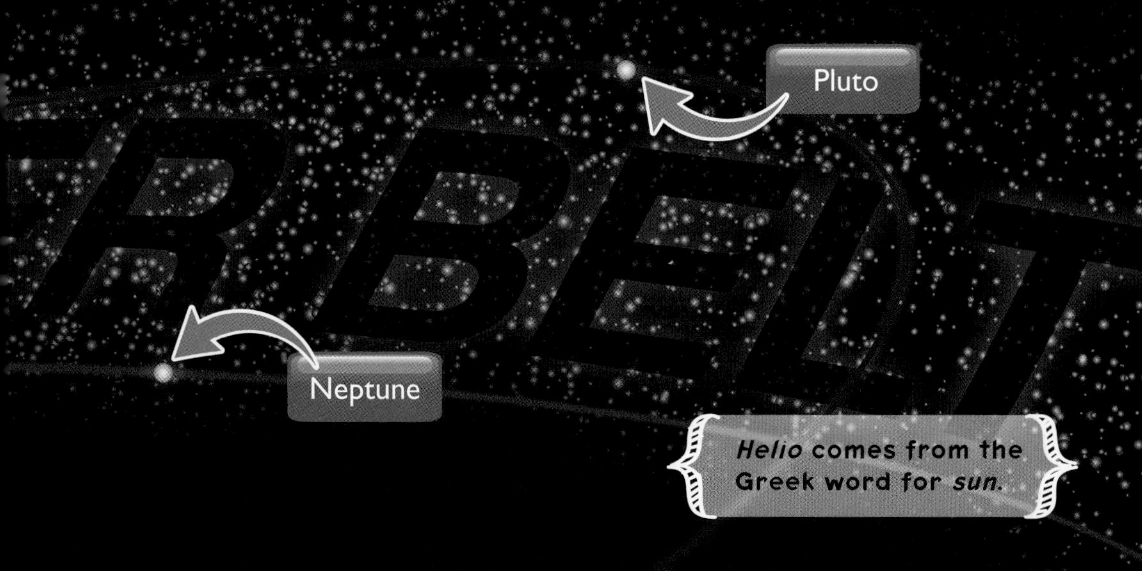

Helio comes from the Greek word for *sun*.

The Sun and the Five Dwarfs

As of 2008, there are five dwarf planets in our solar system. They are Pluto, Eris, Ceres, Haumea (hou-MEY-uh), and Makemake (MAH-keh MAH-keh). All of the dwarf planets except Ceres are located in the Kuiper Belt. Ceres is located in the asteroid belt.

Oort Cloud

Before we go any further, stop and think for a minute. Just how far are we talking? Think of it like this:

To travel by plane across the United States takes about six hours. That is six hours to go across a small area of Earth. If an airplane could fly from the sun to Neptune, it would take about six *million* hours. But even so, that would only be like getting to the first bathroom break on a car trip! You'd still have billions of kilometers and millions of hours to go.

Are you starting to get some idea of how big space is?

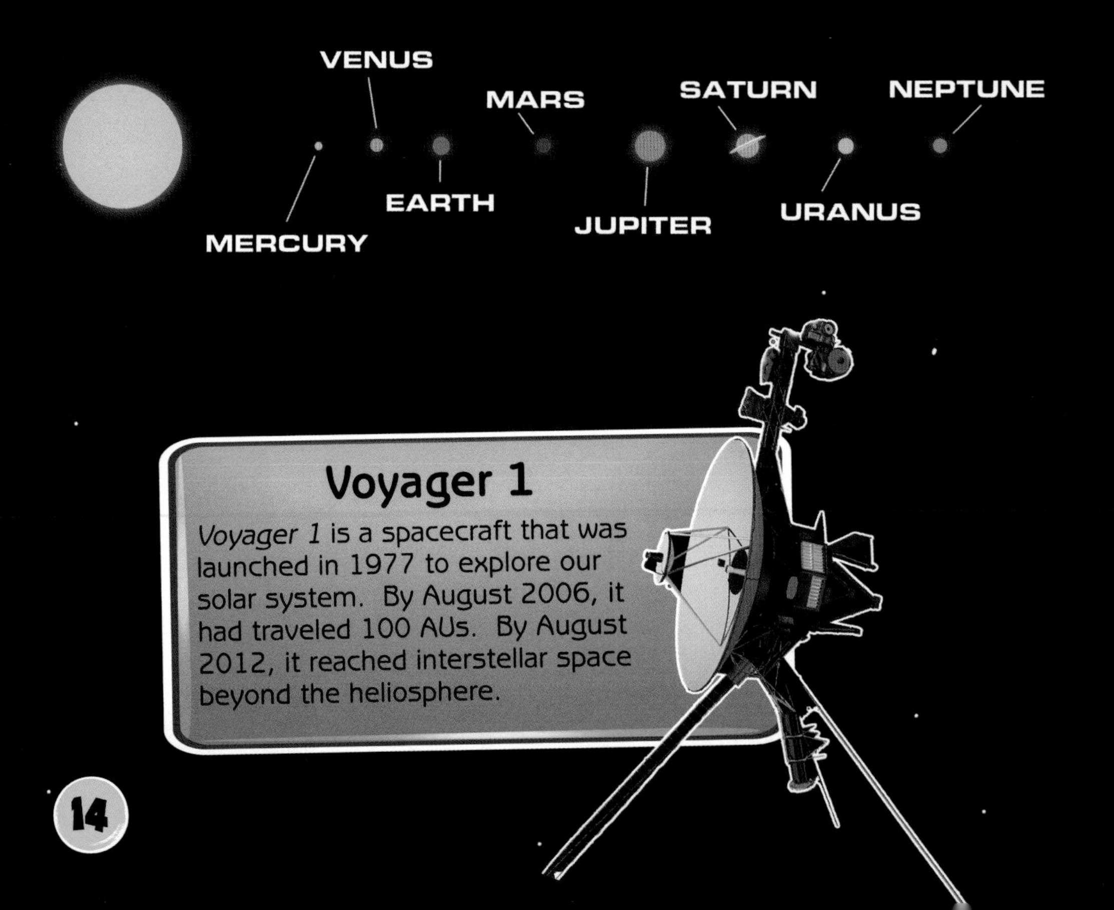

Voyager 1

Voyager 1 is a spacecraft that was launched in 1977 to explore our solar system. By August 2006, it had traveled 100 AUs. By August 2012, it reached interstellar space beyond the heliosphere.

Past the Kuiper Belt, at the far edge of our solar system, is an area we have never visited. We call it the *Oort Cloud.* It extends to 100,000 AUs from the sun! We can't see the Oort Cloud. But it seems to be filled with ice and gases. Sometimes, icy comets travel near Earth. They appear to come from the Oort Cloud.

KUIPER BELT

OORT CLOUD

Jan Oort

The Oort Cloud is named for Jan Oort (yawn ohrt), a Dutch astronomer who made a lot of important studies about the Milky Way and predicted the existence of the Oort Cloud.

Putting It Together

All the areas talked about so far are part of our solar system. They're within our sun's pull. The sun's gravity is greatest within about 126,000 AUs. That's about half as far as it is to the next closest star.

Many other stars in our galaxy have their own **planetary system.** That's an area in which planets and other bodies orbit a star. Some of those planets are larger than Earth. Some are smaller. Some of those planets have moons.

In our galaxy alone, there are at least 200 billion stars. But there are billions more galaxies in the universe. There may be billions of other solar systems, too.

With all those stars, it makes a person wonder. What are the odds that there is another planet like Earth orbiting another sun?

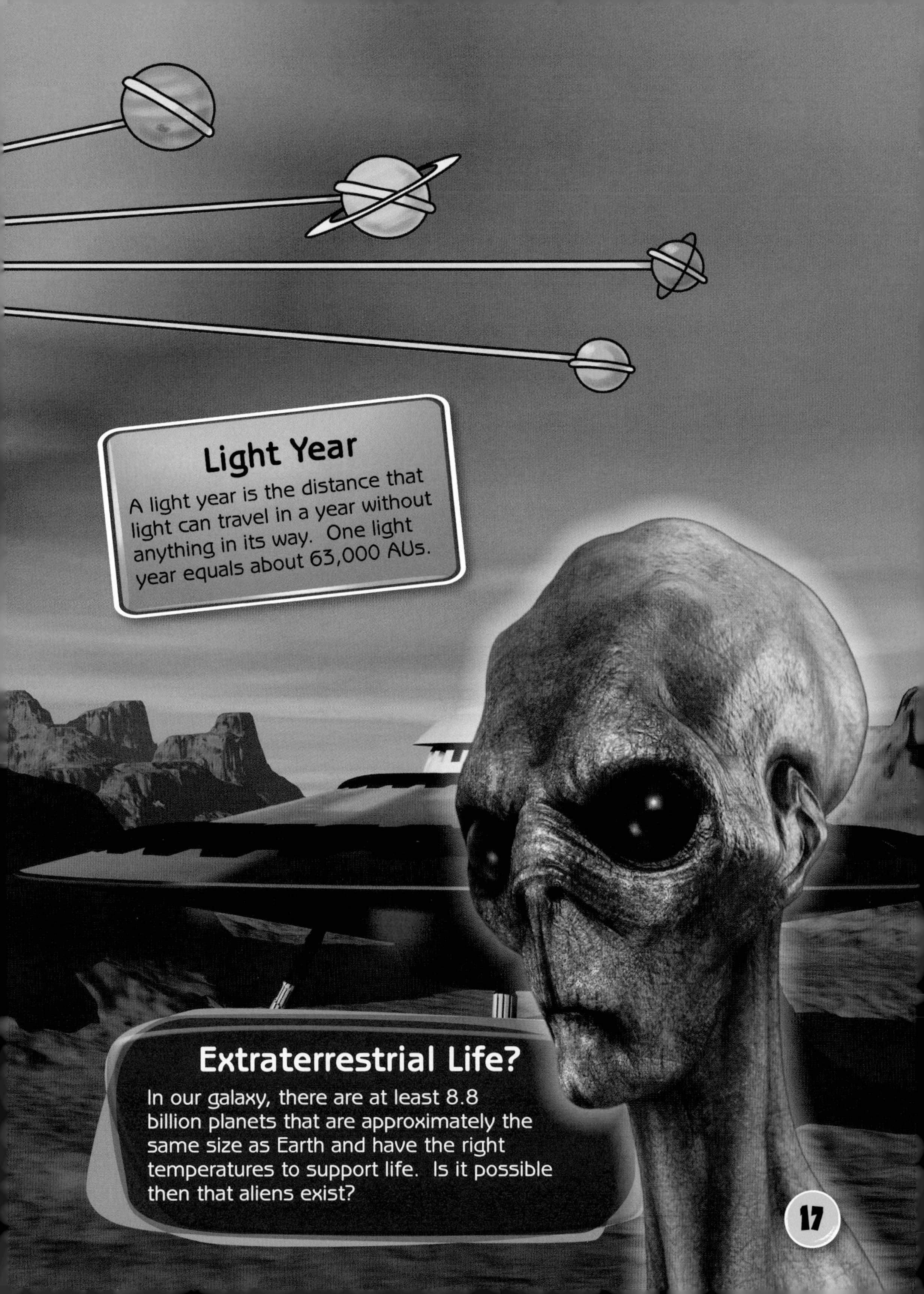
Light Year
A light year is the distance that
light can travel in a year without
anything in its way. One light
year equals about 63,000 AUs.
Extraterrestrial Life?
In our galaxy, there are at least 8.8
billion planets that are approximately the
same size as Earth and have the right
temperatures to support life. Is it possible
then that aliens exist?

Beyond Our Solar System

In all of space, our solar system is like a tiny spot on a tiny bug that an enormous elephant steps on and never notices. Really, it's not even a spot. It's more like a speck on the spot on the bug!

Sometimes, it's impossible for that bug to realize just how much more there is to the world than the bug can see. The world is so large, and the bug is so small. *We* can be like that bug. The universe is larger than we can even imagine.

The Milky Way

Past the edges of our solar system are more stars and planets. The stars form a pattern. It looks like a toy pinwheel. On each arm of the pinwheel are millions and even billions of stars. Our sun is one star way up on one of those arms. Earth is there, too, of course. The pinwheel is called the *Milky Way galaxy*.

The nearest star system beyond our solar system is *Alpha Centauri*. It's about 4.4 light years away, or about 275,000 AUs.

Mysterious Matter

Most of the mass in the Milky Way comes from a mysterious substance called *dark matter*. Dark matter is a material that exists in space that we are unable to see.

our sun

The Milky Way is called a spiral galaxy because of its shape.

Many of the stars on the pinwheel have their own planetary systems. We already know about thousands of these planets. More are being found all the time. All these planets and stars are part of the Milky Way. Our solar system is one tiny part of the galaxy. And Earth is just a tiny dot.

In the Milky Way, each planet orbits its star. But each star orbits something, too. The stars orbit a large **black hole** at the center of the galaxy. The name is a little misleading. A black hole isn't really a hole, and it's not really empty. It's a bunch of **matter** that's packed together very tightly. Its strong gravity won't let anything escape. Even light can't escape. The black hole at the heart of the Milky Way is 4 million times larger than our sun. But don't worry! It's 1,764 million AUs from our planet. We're safe from its gravity!

Like dark matter, scientists can't see black holes. But they can see the effects of their gravity and estimate where they're located.

artist's concept of a black hole

*Sagittarius A** (pronounced Sagittarius A-Star) is the name of a black hole in the center of the Milky Way galaxy.

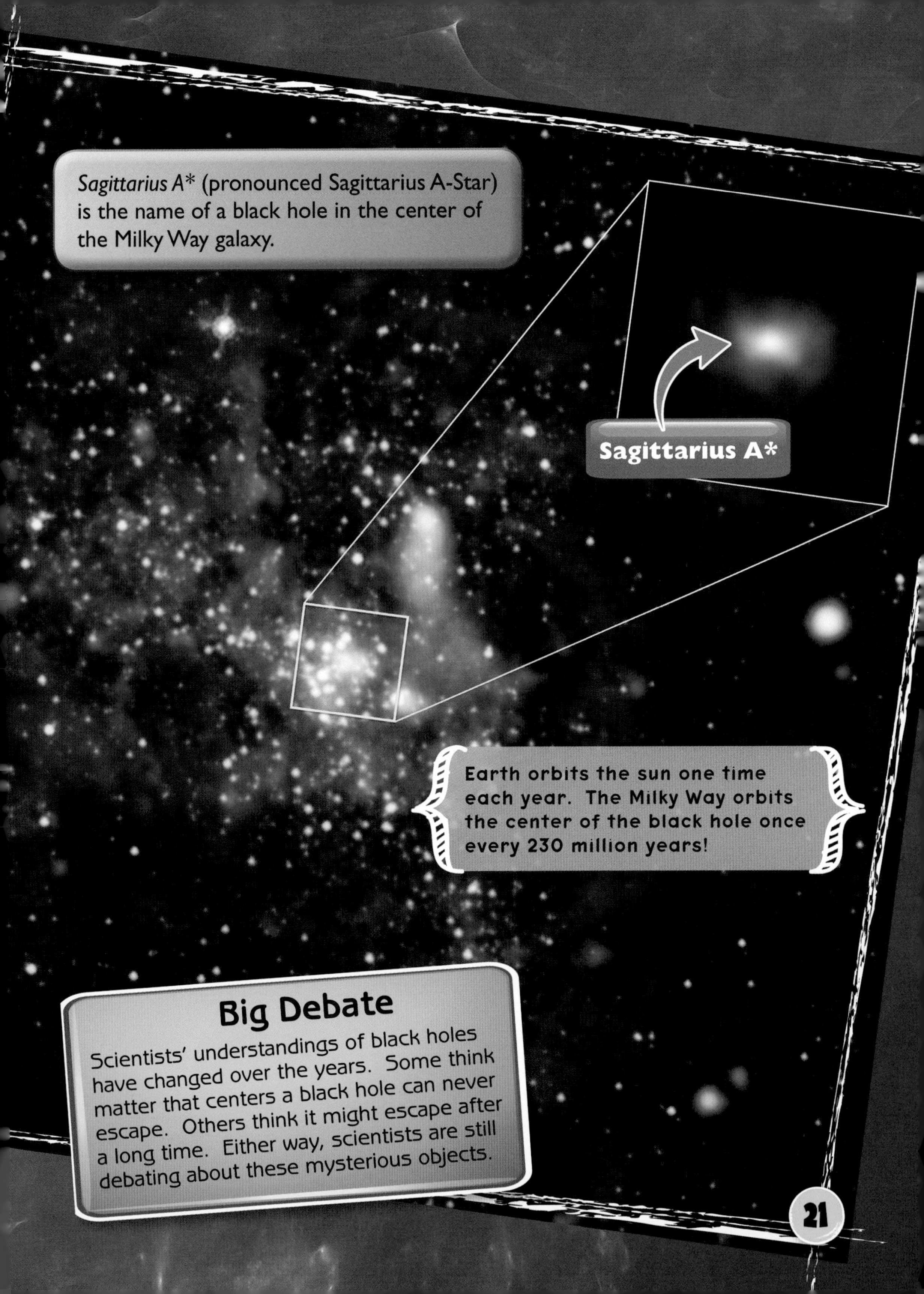

Earth orbits the sun one time each year. The Milky Way orbits the center of the black hole once every 230 million years!

Big Debate

Scientists' understandings of black holes have changed over the years. Some think matter that centers a black hole can never escape. Others think it might escape after a long time. Either way, scientists are still debating about these mysterious objects.

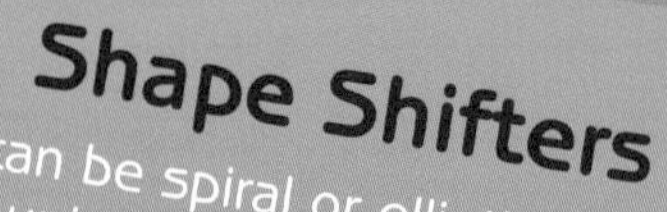

Shape Shifters

Galaxies can be spiral or elliptical, or they may have unique shapes like sticks or rings.

Elliptical galaxies are shaped like a stretched-out sphere. When we look at them in the sky, they look like ovals.

Two-thirds of all galaxies are spiral. Our own Milky Way is a spiral galaxy! They have a bulge in the center, a disk around the bulge, and a halo.

Lenticular (len-TIK-yuh-ler) galaxies are like a spiral galaxy, with a bulge and a disk. They don't have the same spiral shape though!

Irregular galaxies don't fit the other types and usually don't have a pattern.

The Milky Way is just one galaxy in a group of about 30 large galaxies. Together, they are called the *Local Group*.

All the galaxies in the Local Group orbit a center of gravity. The center is somewhere between the Milky Way and the Andromeda galaxies.

Of course, the Local Group is huge. It's 630 billion AUs from end to end. (That's the same as 10 million light years.) And the Local Group is just one of many groups of galaxies in the universe. Each group orbits its own center.

One way that we know the universe is expanding is how the galaxies move. All the groups are moving away from one another.

Always Changing, Always Growing

We don't have to look far to know that the universe is always changing. Each body in space revolves around a center. So, everything is moving. We can tell, too, that the universe is always expanding.

In recent years, people have learned how to send machines into space. There are telescopes out there. There are cameras, too. Satellites orbit Earth and study space. Spacecrafts such as *Voyager 1* are sent into deep space. They're sent to collect information and then to send it back to us. They carry information, too. That way, if they meet other beings in space, they can tell them about us.

Navigate Space

You can go online to **www.nasa.gov** to see videos and images of space explorations. You can even watch live video of space!

Our Eye in the Sky

The Hubble Space Telescope was aimed at a single area in space for about 12 days. Even though the area was smaller than the full moon, nearly 10,000 galaxies were found there!

Scientists have learned a lot about space. But what we know is just a tiny fraction of all there is to know. We have seen a lot of space. But what we have seen is just a tiny fraction of all there is to see. The more we learn, the more we realize there is to learn!

One thing we know is that it's possible for other planetary systems to grow and support life. With all the billions of stars and planets, it only makes sense that somewhere out there, life has developed. Even so, we have not found signs of life anywhere other than on Earth.

Not yet, that is!

"Is there
anybody
out there?"

Think Like a Scientist

How big is our solar system? Experiment and find out!

What to Get

- 1 large yellow bead
- 7 meters (7.7 yards) of string
- 8 small beads of different colors
- meter stick
- scissors

What to Do

1. Imagine that 10 centimeters = 1 AU. Find and convert the AU distance of each planet, the heliosphere, and the Oort Cloud.

Celestial body	AU
Mercury	0.4
Venus	0.7
Earth	1.0
Mars	1.5
Jupiter	5.2
Saturn	9.6
Uranus	19.2
Neptune	30
Heliosphere	50
Oort Cloud	100,000

2. Cut eight pieces of string to match the scale distances. You may need to add 4 cm to each string to accommodate knot tying. (Hint: Earth's distance = 1 AU = 10 cm.)

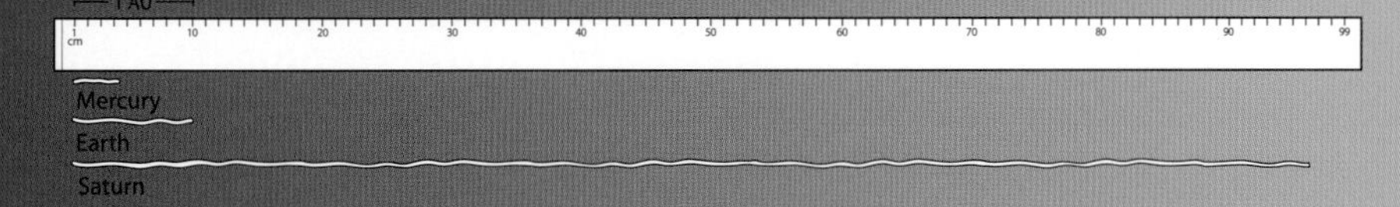

3. Tie the eight strings to the yellow bead, which represents the sun. Decide which of the small beads represents each planet. Tie each bead to a string to represent the eight planets.

4. Find a large open space. Hold the yellow bead. Have eight other people hold each of the other beads.

Mars
Earth
Venus
Mercury
Sun

5. How far away would someone have to stand to represent the heliosphere and the Oort Cloud? What does that tell you about the size of your solar system?

Glossary

black hole—an area in space with gravity so strong that light cannot escape

classified—arranged in groups with similar things

dwarf planets—objects in space that orbit a star but have not cleared their orbits of other objects

expanding—increasing in size, range, or amount

gravity—a force that acts between objects, pulling one toward the other

infinity—a space, amount, or period of time that has no limits or end

matter—anything that has mass and takes up space

orbit—the curved path an object follows as it goes around something else

planetary system—a group of planets and other bodies orbiting a central star

revolve—to move around something in a circular path

satellites—objects in space that orbit other larger objects

universe—everything in space

Index

*Conversions from p.29

Planet or Area	cm
Sun	0 cm
Mercury	4 cm
Venus	7 cm
Earth	10 cm
Mars	15 cm
Jupiter	52 cm
Saturn	96 cm
Uranus	192 cm
Neptune	300 cm
Heliosphere	500 cm
Oort Cloud	1,000,000 cm

Your Turn!

Counting Stars

On a very dark night, look up at the stars. How many do you see? There are many more there than you notice at first, and what you see is just the tiniest fraction of all the stars there are. Our planet, and each of us on the planet, is just a small dot in the entire universe!